# Bub Plays Tag

By Sally Cowan

One grey day,
Bub and Pim played tag.
They had great fun!

Big Mag was in his tree.

Then a strong gust of wind made Big Mag's tree sway this way and that.

Hey, Big Mag!
Your tree is not safe!
It will break!

The tree fell sideways.

Big Mag had to fly
out of the way!

The weight of the tree could
crush him!

The tall tree lay flat.

"Where will I stay?" wailed Big Mag.

Big Mag aimed for Bub's branch.

"Can Big Mag stay in this tree?" Bub said to Pim.
"He can sip buds with us!"

"Big Mag does not sip buds,"
said Pim.

"Snails are my prey,"
said Big Mag.
"I like steak, too!"

Big Mag can play tag with us!
May I stay with you, Pim?

"What do you say, Mum?"
said Bub.

"I **love** to play tag!" said Big Mag.
"I am your prey, Bub!"

Bub could not wait!

He gave Big Mag's tail
a little tap.

## CHECKING FOR MEANING

1. What does Big Mag like to eat? *(Literal)*
2. What happened to Big Mag's tree? *(Literal)*
3. How do you think Pim felt about sharing their tree with Big Mag? *(Inferential)*

## EXTENDING VOCABULARY

| | |
|---|---|
| **sway** | Read the word *sway*. What are the sounds in this word? What does *sway* mean? What are some things that can sway? |
| **hey** | When might you use the word *hey*? What other words can you use to get people's attention? |
| **weight** | What is the base of the word *weight*? What can you think of that has a heavy weight? What has a light weight? |

## MOVING BEYOND THE TEXT

1. The birds played tag. What are some other games that you can play outdoors?
2. Big Mag learned that a tree can be a dangerous place to be during a storm. Where should you go during a storm? Why is this place safe?
3. Would you have invited Big Mag to stay on your branch if you were Pim or Bub? Why?
4. Big Mag liked to eat snails and steak. What else might birds eat?

## TIME TO WRITE

Write about how Big Mag felt about Bub's kindness.

# PRACTICE WORDS